Blood Moon—God's Warning

Jewish Feasts and the Blood Moons of 2014 and 2015

AN ESSAY

J. NELL BROWN

ROGUE READS
LLC

J. Nell Brown

Essay: *Blood Moon—God's Warning: Why Knowledge of Jewish Feasts Is Essential to Understand the Blood Moons of 2014 and 2015.*

Copyright © 2014 by J. Nell Brown, LLC (Jeanelle Denise Brown)

All rights reserved. No part of this publication may be reproduced, distributed, or transmitted in any form or by any means, including photocopying, recording, or other electronic or mechanical methods, without the prior written permission of the publisher and author, except in the case of brief quotations embodied in critical reviews and certain other noncommercial uses permitted by copyright law. For permission requests, write to the author at www.JNellBrown.com 'contact us' page.

Scripture passages are taken from the King James Version (KJV) unless noted otherwise.

Published by Rogue Reads, LLC.

For ordering information, contact the publisher via author's website, www.JNellBrown.com.

Printed in the United States of America

*Second Edition, 2014

Blood Moon—God's Warning

Books by

J. Nell Brown

Nonfiction

Shhh, My Father Is Speaking, and I Am Listening: A Bible Study on Hearing God's Voice

Blood Moon—God's Warning: Why Knowledge of Jewish Feasts Is Essential to Understand the Blood Moons of 2014 and 2015

Fiction

God Factor Saga Series EBooks:

A Generation of Lighted Evergreens: A Novella

Frozen Prayers

Blood Moon Relics

Houseguest: A Short Story

Autumn Rains: A Winter Adventure Love Story

The Rose of A.D. 30: A Trilogy

Collector's First Edition Paperback
The Omega Journey: Blood Moons Whisper

Coming January 2016

God Factor Saga Series Book 4: Desert Places

J. Nell Brown

Coming January 2017

God Factor Saga Series Book 5: The Lighthouse Leads

The Tapestry: One American's Story

Blood Moon—God's Warning

CONTENTS

1. A History Lesson	9
2. What Time Is It?	14
3. Jewish Feasts	19
4. Spring Feasts	22
5. Trumpets	28
6. Fall Feasts	31
7. Blood Moons	41
8. Reader's Question	48
Dear Reader ...	54
Frozen Prayers Preview	55
Acknowledgments	57
Author Biography	58

J. Nell Brown

Study of Blood Moons and Jewish Feasts

What do the dates below have in common?

The Spanish Inquisition—1492

* Passover, April 2, 1493
* Sukkoth, September 25, 1493
* Passover, March 22, 1494
* Sukkoth, September 15, 1494

The Israeli War of Independence—1948

* Passover, April 13, 1949
* Sukkoth, October 7, 1949
* Passover, April 2, 1950
* Sukkoth, September 26, 1950

The Arab-Israeli Six-Day War—1967

* Passover, April 24, 1967
* Sukkoth, October. 18, 1967
* Passover, April 13, 1968
* Sukkoth, October 6, 1968

Current blood moons

* Passover, April 15, 2014
* Sukkoth, October 8, 2014
* Passover, April 4, 2015
* Sukkoth, September 28, 2015

Blood Moon—God's Warning

Follow J. Nell Brown as she whets your appetite for knowledge about a significant event in astronomy called a tetrad of blood moons. She will share with you a concise body of research she compiled to write her first novel, *The Omega Journey ~ Blood Moons Whisper*.

Astronomy is the study of the sky and is not astrology. God uses the sky to tell of His plans. "The heavens declare the glory of God; and the firmament sheweth his handywork" (Psalms 19:1). "And God said, Let there be lights in the firmament of the heaven to divide the day from the night; and let them be for signs, and for seasons, and for days, and years" (Genesis 1:14).

Gentiles follow the Gregorian calendar. Could the historical change from the Hebrew calendar to the Gregorian one be instigated by Satan, the deceiver of mankind? "And he shall speak great words against the most High, and shall wear out the saints of the most High, and think to **change times and laws**: and they shall be given into his hand until a time and times and the dividing of time" (Daniel 7:25). The prophet Daniel records this scripture as he refers to the spirit of antichrist—the spirit that wars against God and His plans. Since the Garden of Eden, the spirit of antichrist has sought to deceive mankind into worshiping Satan. Thus, it is no surprise that the spirit of antichrist belongs to Satan!

Look at the list of dates on the previous page and note the patterns.

There are three trends. First, each time period represents a point in history when a significant event affected the Jewish people.

J. Nell Brown

Second, each period is a group of four known as a tetrad. Third, each order of dates follows the same pattern of holidays: Passover, Sukkoth, Passover, and Sukkoth.

Follow along as J. Nell Brown takes you on a journey through Jewish feasts and blood moons, exploring how they may apply to humanity and God's plans.

"But this is that which was spoken by the prophet Joel; And it shall come to pass in the last days, saith God, I will pour out of my Spirit upon all flesh: and your sons and your daughters shall prophesy, and your young men shall see visions, and your old men shall dream dreams: And on my servants and on my handmaidens I will pour out in those days of my Spirit; and they shall prophesy: And I will shew wonders in heaven above, and signs in the earth beneath; blood, and fire, and vapour of smoke: The sun shall be turned into darkness, and the moon into blood, before the great and notable day of the Lord come: And it shall come to pass, that whosoever shall call on the name of the Lord shall be saved" (Acts 2:16-21).

Chapter 1

A History Lesson

History . . .

The moment I speak this word, someone's eyes will glaze over and another will sit up in his seat and anticipate my next sentence. I'm a history buff, so I would do the latter.

My mother is a retired middle school teacher. Many times, she would say, "These kids don't know how good they have it. If they knew their history, they would appreciate their present opportunities and would learn how to arrive at their future destination."

My mom was right and still is.

Christians can be accused of not knowing our history. We forget that our faith was birthed from the Abrahamic Covenant, which is God's covenant with Abraham. As a result, many Christians fall prey to weird doctrines, apathy, and apostasy.

The purpose of the Abrahamic Covenant was to repair the fellowship with God man lost in the Garden of Eden after man rejected God's instruction and embraced the advice of the deceiver, Satan.

In order to understand blood moons and the foreshadowing of Jewish feasts, we must immerse ourselves in our early discipleship culture, the Hebrew culture. After remembering our cultural roots, we can grasp a deeper meaning of the times in which we are living.

By the end of this essay, we will have studied our Christian Hebraic history and Biblical truths, and we will secure vital knowledge to arrive at our future victorious.

Let me clarify. The influence of the prosperity gospel in Christendom requires me to clarify my words *victorious future*. My definition of *victory* can be found in Paul's words to Timothy: "I have fought a good fight, I have finished my course, I have kept the faith: Henceforth there is laid up for me a crown of righteousness, which the Lord, the righteous judge, shall give me at that day: and not to me only, but unto all them also that love his appearing" (2 Timothy 4:7-8).

Every Christian should anticipate Jesus's return. If you are a reader who has little desire to see your Messiah, I suggest taking a few days to ask God when your relationship with Jesus became dull. Two lovers anticipate their reunion, so Jesus's church should anticipate His return.

Before Jesus came to earth, God saw two groups of people: Jews and Gentiles. After Jesus fulfilled His mission of dying for the sins of the world and resurrecting from the grave to conquer death, God now sees two different groups of people: those who are a part of the Abrahamic Covenant and those who are not. "There is neither

Blood Moon—God's Warning

Jew nor Greek, there is neither bond nor free, there is neither male nor female: for ye are all one in Christ Jesus" (Galatians 3:28).

The price God paid to include Gentiles in this covenant was enormous. He sacrificed His only Son to bridge the gap between God's righteousness and mankind's sinful nature. "For God so loved the world, that he gave his only begotten Son, that whosoever believeth in him should not perish, but have everlasting life" (John 3:16).

Sin is simply missing the mark. Humans miss the mark every second in our thought life and every minute in our actions.

How did Gentiles become a part of the Abrahamic Covenant? Jesus grafted us into the covenant by His blood.

More than likely, you are reading this essay because you've heard about the 2014-2015 blood moons and Jewish feasts, and you hope that these astronomical sightings indicate that Jesus's return, also known as the rapture, is close. God loves your anticipation.

Remember, as we study Jesus's words from the Bible and His fulfillment of the spring Jewish feasts, and as we anticipate His fulfillment of the fall Jewish feasts, we must remind ourselves that Jesus was Hebrew. His culture was Hebrew. His language was Aramaic. He spoke in idioms from the perspective of His Hebrew culture.

God had to choose a group of people to carry to the world the prophetic call found in the Holy Scriptures. He chose the Hebrews. God is sovereign, so His choice is His prerogative.

What is an idiom? An idiom is a group of words established by usage as having a meaning not deducible from those of the individual words. For example, we know that when we say, "It will rain cats and dogs," that we really mean we are anticipating a heavy rainfall of water and not sweet cuddly mammals!

Jesus spoke much of His New Testament text in parables and idioms.

Remember, Saul, who was inspired to write most of the New Testament, was a Pharisaic Jew. A Pharisee would be equivalent to our culture's most learned scholar of a particular subject. Saul could quote the Torah from memory. He understood his culture. However, the deeper spiritual truths in the Hebrew Scriptures were hidden from Saul until Jesus literally knocked Saul off his donkey, blinded him, and poured spiritual vision and wisdom into his soul. Saul became Paul that day, and Paul was responsible for hearing from God and writing the majority of the New Testament. May we not be so learned that Jesus must knock us off our donkey to understand His spiritual message!

All of Jesus's disciples were Jewish.

Are you getting my point?

I think you are.

Allow yourself to become a Hebrew during this study. Set your cultural understandings aside, and let's enjoy the journey together.

I don't like predictions because I trust God in my daily life.

Blood Moon—God's Warning

God knows the details, but we are directed in scripture to "watch and pray" for Jesus's return.

Let's dig into a deeper meaning of Jewish feasts and blood moons. You'll close this eBook with more excitement for Jesus's return.

Chapter 2
What Time Is It?

Gentiles follow the Gregorian calendar. Could the historical change from the Hebrew calendar to the Gregorian one be instigated by Satan?

"And he shall speak great words against the most High, and shall wear out the saints of the most High, and **think to change** times and laws: and they shall be given into his hand until a time and times and the dividing of time" (Daniel 7:25).

The prophet Daniel records this scripture as he refers to the spirit of antichrist, the spirit that wars against God and His plans.

The Gregorian calendar is a reformed Julian calendar, and it is also called the Western or Christian calendar. The Gregorian calendar is the most widely used civil calendar and has been the unofficial global standard for decades.

The calendar was introduced and named by Pope Gregory XIII on February 24, 1582. The human motivation for the adjustment of the Julian calendar was to bring the date for the celebration of Easter to the time of year in which the First Council of Nicaea had agreed upon. In A.D. 325, the First Council of

Blood Moon—God's Warning

Nicaea established the date of Easter as the first Sunday after the full moon (the Paschal Full Moon) following the March equinox.

Because the celebration of Easter was tied to the spring equinox, the Roman Catholic Church considered this steady drift of Easter's date undesirable.

Using the Gregorian calendar, Easter always falls on a Sunday between March 22nd and April 25th and within about seven days after the astronomical full moon.

As you can deduce, Easter has nothing to do with Passover, the Jewish feast concurring with Jesus's crucifixion. How unfortunate!

Oftentimes humans believe their motivations to be pure. The change from the Hebrew lunar-solar calendar to the Gregorian calendar may have been another deceptive tool Satan used to confuse the masses in regards to important dates in God's calendar, the Hebrew calendar.

The Hebrew calendar is a lunar-solar calendar. The months are based upon lunar cycles, and the years are based on solar cycles.

The order of months is as follows:

Month 1: Nisan (March)

Month 2: Iyar (April)

Month 3: Sivan (May)

Month 4: Tamuz (June)

Month 5: Av (July)

Month 6: Elul (August)

Month 7: Tishri (September)

Month 8: Cheshran (October)

Month 9: Kislev (November)

Month 10: Terat (December)

Month 11: Shevat (January)

Month 12: Adar I (February)

Month 13: Adar II (leap year)

The current year of the Hebrew calendar, 5774, is a leap year, so Adar II will be added to the Hebrew calendar in the Gregorian year 2015.

We will have difficulty in understanding the blood moons of 2014 and 2015 if we do not understand what year we are in on the Hebrew calendar. This Hebrew year, 5774, is the Gregorian calendar year 2014, and 5775 is the Gregorian calendar year 2015.

The Hebrew sacred (religious) calendar starts with the Gregorian calendar month of March and ends twelve to thirteen months later.

All Jewish feasts are calculated from the first day of the month of Nisan. The flex in months between a twelve or thirteen month year corresponds to the Hebrew leap year. Read Leviticus 23 to understand when and why God instructed Moses to incorporate a sacred start of the New Year into their civil calendar.

The civil calendar starts in Tishri with Rosh Hashanah. Ancient Judeans believed God created the world during the month of Tishri. The Hebrew civil calendar starts with the Gregorian calendar month of September or October and ends twelve to thirteen months later. The feast that starts the Hebrew civil year is

Blood Moon—God's Warning

called Rosh Hashanah or the New Year and is known as the Feast of Trumpets in Christendom.

If you think about the Gregorian calendar, it is not unusual to have two different annual cycles like we see in the Hebrew calendar. Western culture refers to the New Year in January and a fiscal year in July, etc.

On a side note, there are actually four different annual cycles in the Hebrew calendar. The other two cycles are important for the animal tithe practiced in ancient times and the tree offering. We will focus only on the religious and civil year annual cycles.

Next, we must relearn how to read a clock in order to make sense of the following study.

The Western day starts in the morning at 00:00 in military time, which correlates with midnight.

The Western day ends at 23:59, or 11:59 pm.

The spirit of antichrist has moved us even farther away from an understanding of God's calendar by changing the way most people process time.

Remember, we are Hebrew for the purpose of this study, so let's take a look at our history.

The Hebrew clock begins in the evening at sundown, and this clock is Biblically accurate. "And God said, Let there be light: and there was light. And God saw the light, that it was good: and God divided the light from the darkness. And God called the light Day, and the darkness he called Night. **And the evening and the morning were the first day**" (Genesis 1:3-5).

Wow!

We start our day at midnight; however, God starts His day in the evening around 18:00, or 6:00 pm for those who don't process the day in military time.

No wonder the average Christian has a hard time understanding how Jesus fulfilled the spring Jewish feasts with His first arrival on earth! Our calendar and our watches are all set to different times.

Chapter 3
Jewish Feasts

Now, since we have reviewed the errors of the Gregorian calendar and clock, let's start to unravel the mysteries hidden in Jewish feasts.

Western Christians often think of food when I mention the word *feasts*. Once again, we are Hebrews for the purpose of this book. The word *feasts* in Hebrew means "God's appointed time."

Let's pause. God is an event driven God. From the very beginning, He created the world. After the fall of mankind, He created a plan to restore our broken fellowship with Him. This plan started with the Old Testament prophets and their prophecies. "Therefore the Lord himself shall give you a sign; Behold, a virgin shall conceive, and bear a son, and shall call his name Immanuel" (Isaiah 7:14).

These prophecies continued until Jesus arrived on the scene. The shepherds were led by angels to the manger of a babe wrapped in swaddling clothes. The wise men were guided by the northern star.

All of the feasts discussed in Exodus 12 and Leviticus 23 are a foreshadowing of God's plan to redeem mankind. Leviticus 23 spells out each feast and grouping of events that Jesus would fulfill to complete His redemptive plan of providing a path for man to be reconciled to God.

If you are like me, you may be thinking what interesting clues could possibly be found in Leviticus. Patience. There are many exciting clues. Let's go and discover them.

There are two major categories of Jewish feasts: the Spring Feasts and the Fall Feasts.

The Spring Feasts in Leviticus 23 were a foreshadowing of the first coming of the Messiah, Jesus. Paul gives more clarification in regards to the purpose of Jewish feasts. "Therefore do not let anyone judge you by what you eat or drink, or with regard to a religious festival, a New Moon celebration or a Sabbath day. These are a shadow of the things that were to come; the reality, however, is found in Christ" (Colossians 2:16-17 NIV).

The Fall Feasts in Leviticus 23 were a foreshadowing of the second coming of Jesus the Messiah. His second coming will begin with the rapture of the church. We will talk about this soon.

Review this scripture passage with me. "Then shall we know, if we follow on to know the Lord: his going forth is prepared as the morning; and he shall come unto us as the rain, as the latter and former rain unto the earth" (Hosea 6:3).

There are two seasons of rain in Israel, the former rain and the latter rain. Once again, in order to dig deeper we must become Hebrew and reflect on the Jewish idiom structure of this sentence. The rains refer to a spiritual rain. The Hebrew word for *rain* in this passage means "teacher." Jesus was referred to in the scriptures as

Blood Moon—God's Warning

Master, which is another word for "teacher." Thus, the former rains denote Jesus's first appearance on earth, and the latter rains denote Jesus's second appearance on earth.

There are seven Jewish feasts. A study of numerology in the Bible reminds us that *seven* means "completion." The seven days of creation represent God's complete creation; the seven candlesticks in the Revelation represent the complete church. The seven Jewish feasts delineate that God has foreshadowed His **complete** plan of redemption. God doesn't need imperfect man adding another step to His perfect plan. Unfortunately, many religions try to!

Chapter 4

Spring Feasts

For the purpose of this study, I am going to order the months based on the sacred Hebrew calendar, where the first month is Nisan. Why? God told Moses to begin their year in Nisan and to count the start dates of the following feasts from the first day of Nisan.

The **Feast of Passover (Pesach)** is celebrated on the fourteenth day of Nisan. Jews enslaved by the Egyptians were the first to observe Passover. God instructed Moses in Egypt, "This month shall be your beginning of months; it shall be the first month of the year to you. Speak to all the congregation of Israel, saying: 'On the **tenth** of this month, Nisan, every man shall take for himself a lamb…Your lamb shall be without blemish, a male of the first year… Now you shall keep it until the **fourteenth** day of the same month. Then the whole assembly of the congregation of Israel shall kill it at twilight" (Exodus 12:2-6 NKJV).

After God gave Moses these instructions, and the Hebrews followed them, a death angel killed the first born in any house in Egypt not marked with lamb's blood. The application of the lamb's

Blood Moon—God's Warning

blood to the doorpost represented Jesus applying His blood to a wooden cross.

Review the scripture passage above. Each household acquired a lamb on the tenth day, but the lamb was not sacrificed until the fourteenth day. What is the significance of this four-day wait? Jesus entered Jerusalem on the tenth day of Nisan, entered the temple, and was observed by the Hebrews and Romans. He would be sacrificed on the fourteenth day at the same time the Passover lamb was killed in Exodus 12. As a result, Exodus 12 was a foreshadowing of when the Messiah would die.

If we time travel from 1400 BC when Leviticus was written to AD 33 when Jesus was taken outside of the city gate to Golgotha to be crucified, you will discover Jesus was crucified the same hour that the people would take a sacrificial lamb outside the temple gate and kill it for the sins of the people. Exodus 12:6 tells us that the lamb would be killed on the fourteenth day at twilight.

It is time for another Hebrew understanding of our clock. *Twilight* means "between the evenings." Remember the Hebrew day begins at sundown, 6:00 pm, and ends the next evening at sundown, 6:00 pm. The Hebrew clock refers to times as a function of hours (i.e., the ninth hour, which would be 3:00 pm).

The Hebrew day is split into twelve-hour increments, evening (6:00 pm to 6:00 am) and morning (6:00 am to 6:00 pm).

We know Jesus died before the Sabbath. Let's focus on the twelve-hour increment of 6:00 am to 6:00 pm. The twelve-hour morning is further divided into six-hour blocks for ease of computing time. The first block is 6:00 am to 12:00 pm, noon. The second block is 12:00 pm to 6:00 pm. The middle point of the second block is 3:00 pm, also known as the ninth hour. "Between the evenings" would be 3:00 pm. Jesus died at 3:00 pm; just as the lamb sacrificed in Exodus was killed at 3:00 pm.

Jesus gave His life as the final and perfect Passover sacrifice. He fulfilled the prophetic foreshadowing of this feast with His death.

The **Feast of Unleavened Bread** is the second spring feast. It follows one day after Passover, on the fifteenth day of Nisan.

Another Hebrew time check is necessary. The Hebrew day begins at sundown, or 6:00 pm. Jesus would need to be in the tomb before the Sabbath because a burial would be considered a form of work. No work was to be done on the Sabbath. As a result, Jesus was buried on the 15th day, sometime before the sun went down.

In the Jewish culture, leaven represents sin. After Passover, unleavened bread is prepared and hidden for three days. When Jesus was placed in the tomb for three days, He fulfilled the prophetic foreshadowing of this feast with His burial. He was indeed without sin, and just as leaven within bread represents sin, the Feast of Unleavened Bread utilizes bread without leaven.

Jesus demonstrated that bread represented His body. This symbolism was established when He shared communion with His disciples and said, "This is my body broken for you." As He broke a piece of unleavened bread, He told the multitudes that He was the "Bread of Life."

Blood Moon—God's Warning

The **Feast of First Fruits (Bikkurim)** is the third spring feast. It follows one day after unleavened bread and is celebrated on the sixteenth day of Nisan. This feast represents Jesus rising from the dead and becoming the first of His body who rise from their sleep. "But now is Christ risen from the dead, and become the firstfruits of them that slept" (I Corinthians 15:20).

The Hebrew people were commanded to bring a sheaf of wheat to the priest. A sheaf in Hebrew culture also represents a person. A person must come to the High Priest, Jesus, for salvation.

There are other historically significant events that occurred on the sixteenth day of Nisan: Noah's ark rested on Mt. Ararat; Israel crossed the Red Sea; Israel ate of the first fruits of the Promised Land; and Haman, a persecutor of the Hebrew people, was hanged.

On a side note, first fruits offerings received in many churches probably do not correlate with this feast. For starters, the timing of most preachers' requests for a first fruits offering is January. The Feast of First Fruits would have been in March, or Nisan.

Secondly, Jesus has already fulfilled the feast. As a result, there is nothing for us to fulfill. There is only one meal Jesus asked His followers to celebrate, and that is Communion.

The fourth spring feast is **Pentecost**, also named Shavuot, or the **Feast of Weeks**. Moses instructed the Israelites in Leviticus 23:15-16 when and how to celebrate this feast. "And you shall count for yourselves from the day after the Sabbath, from the day that you brought the sheaf of the wave offering: seven Sabbaths shall be completed. Count fifty days to the day after the seventh Sabbath; then, you shall offer a new grain offering to the Lord." (NKJV)

The grain offering was most likely two loaves of leavened bread. Why does this matter? Leaven represents sin in the ancient Hebrew culture and was forbidden during the Passover meal of bitter herbs and unleavened bread. The Passover bread, as we discussed above, represents Jesus's sinless body.

Pentecost represents the birth of Israel, a nation governed by the law of Yahweh. However, Israel was made up of flawed people. Pentecost also represents the birth of the church and filling of the Holy Spirit. Likewise, just as Israel is full of sinful people, the church is full of those who miss the mark. This is why the two loaves offered during Pentecost are leavened.

I have assumed that readers know the meaning of leavened. Leaven is the yeast that makes bread rise!

After Jesus was raised from the dead, He commanded the disciples to not depart from Jerusalem but to wait for the Promise of the Father. "You shall be baptized with the Holy Spirit not many days from now" (Acts 1:5).

Pentecost does not have a fixed date on the Hebrew calendar because it is counted from the Feast of First Fruits, or the sheaf wave offering.

The Hebrews counted fifty days after the sheaf offering, and Pentecost began.

God gave Moses and the Hebrews the Ten Commandments fifty days after the sheaf offering.

Blood Moon—God's Warning

Fifty days after Jesus's resurrection, the Holy Spirit baptized one hundred twenty disciples with His power. The disciples performed signs and wonders through the Holy Spirit's power.

Pentecost also represents a betrothal contract.

A betrothal contract is foreign to most Westerners. It was a written statement between a man and a woman that they were married but did not physically live together. When we study Rosh Hashanah, you will see the spiritual consummation of the marriage between Jesus and His church.

A betrothal contract was legally binding, and the only way to break it was divorce. We see a betrothal contract playing out in the New Testament after Joseph finds out Mary is pregnant, and they have not consummated their marriage. Joseph planned to divorce Mary, thereby breaking his betrothal contract, until Gabriel, God's angel, told Joseph not to divorce Mary because she was pregnant with the Messiah, Jesus.

In ancient Judean times during Pentecost, God betrothed Himself to Israel. During Pentecost in the New Testament, Jesus betrothed Himself to His church through the Holy Spirit. We will have fullness of our "marriage" to Jesus when He returns and when we physically dwell with Him in Heaven. "And if I go and prepare a place for you, I will come again, and receive you unto myself; that where I am, there ye may be also" (John 14:3).

Chapter 5

Trumpets

The music starts, but probably not the music you are thinking of.

If we want to understand the fall feasts, we must understand the importance of the ram's horn that is used during fall feasts.

There are three trumpets of God separated by time: the first trump, the last trump, and the great trump.

The first trump correlates with the ram's horn tangled in the bush during Abraham's story in Genesis. God asked Abraham to sacrifice his long-awaited son, Isaac. God abhorred child sacrifice practiced in the pagan cultures surrounding Abraham. However, Abraham obeyed and ascended a mountain with firewood, fire, and Isaac. Right before Abraham would have sacrificed his most precious son, God told Abraham to stop and provided him a substitute sacrifice in a bush.

"And Abraham lifted up his eyes, and looked, and behold behind him a ram caught in a thicket by his horns: and Abraham went and took the ram, and offered him up for a burnt offering in the stead of his son" (Genesis 22:13).

Back to the music.

Blood Moon—God's Warning

During the Feast of Pentecost, the first trump is blown through a ram's left horn to signify God's betrothal to Israel.

The last trump is blown through a ram's right horn during Rosh Hashanah in the month of Tishri, September. Yom Teruah is the scriptural name for Rosh Hashanah, meaning the "day of the awakening."

"Speak unto the children of Israel, saying, In the seventh month, in the first day of the month, shall ye have a sabbath, a memorial of blowing of trumpets, an holy convocation" (Leviticus 23:24). Remember, the seventh month is Tishri.

"Behold, I shew you a mystery; We shall not all sleep, but we shall all be changed, In a moment, in the twinkling of an eye, at the **last trump**: for the trumpet shall sound, and the dead shall be raised incorruptible, and we shall be changed" (I Corinthians 15:51-52). We will discuss this scripture in detail later in the study.

The season of Teshuvah is in Jewish culture. The word *Teshuvah* means "to repent." This season begins on the first day of the month of Elul, our August, and continues for forty days until the beginning of Yom Kippur on the tenth day of Tishri, our September.

Thirty days into this season of "repenting," Rosh Hashanah begins. Every morning during this thirty day period, the priest blows a ram's horn to remind the Jewish people to repent.

What is the purpose for the priest blowing the ram's horn? The purpose is to remind the people to repent **before** Rosh Hashanah, or they will find themselves in the Days of Awe, the tribulation period.

J. Nell Brown

After Rosh Hashanah begins, ten days remain until Yom Kippur. These ten days are known as the High Holy Days or Awesome Days. The Sabbath that falls during these ten days is known as Shabbat Shuvah, or the Sabbath of the Return.

Remember, the traditional Jewish Sabbath falls on the Gregorian calendar day of Saturday, not Sunday.

Five days after Yom Kippur, Sukkut, known as the Feast of Tabernacles, follows.

Chapter 6
Fall Feasts

Some could argue that Rosh Hashanah, known as the Feast of Trumpets, is the most important feast for the church at the end of times. This feast is celebrated at the beginning of the month of Tishri, our September.

It is important to note that the Feast of Trumpets is the only feast that falls on the first day of the month in which it happens. All of the other Jewish feasts fall within their respective Jewish months.

The Feast of Trumpets falling on the first of day of the month would surprise the ancient Hebrews, since they could not calculate the beginning day of this feast.

All of the previous feasts and remaining feasts are calculated from the new moon of Nisan. After the new moon is established, one would count fourteen evenings to celebrate Passover, fifteen days to celebrate the Feast of Unleavened Bread, etc.

Why is the moon the astronomical focus of the Hebrew calendar and not the sun? The Hebrew calendar follows the lunar cycle, not the solar cycle like the Gregorian calendar. Each month begins with the new moon. Before telescopes and other gadgets, two watchmen would study the skies for a first glimmer of the new moon. As soon as slivers of light were seen at the edge of a waning darkened disk of the moon, two witnesses would run to the chief of the Sanhedrin and report that they had seen the new moon. The chief would verify their findings. If he agreed, he would declare, "Rosh Chodesh is sanctified, sanctified, sanctified!"

Translated, this would mean that the "new moon was sanctified," and the new month would begin.

Then, watchmen would run over the hillside from east to west similar to a lightning bolt. During their journey, they would light torches notifying the Hebrew community that the chief had declared a new moon and new month. The celebration of Rosh Hashanah, the Feast of Trumpets, would begin.

The Feast of Trumpets represents the rapture of the church. Our word *rapture* comes from the Greek word *harpazo*, which means "to catch away or pluck."

During this feast, many themes are celebrated: resurrection, repentance, kingship, coronation, and marriage.

What are the clues left by the themes included in Rosh Hashanah? Why does Rosh Hashanah correlate with the rapture of the church?

Below are the clues Jesus left His disciples.

Clue 1 is found in Matthew 24:27, "For as the lightning cometh out of the east, and shineth even unto the west; so shall also the coming of the Son of man be."

Blood Moon—God's Warning

Remember, after the new moon was sanctified, the watchman would run and light fires on the hills from the east to the west to notify the people.

When Jesus speaks of a flash of lightning from the east to the west, He is referring to the rapid nature of the rapture as well, leaving another clue to His disciples as to which feast the rapture will fulfill.

Clue 2 is found in Matthew 24:36-44. Many Christians stop at a superficial understanding of this scripture, "But of that day and hour knoweth no man, no, not the angels of heaven, but my Father only . . . Watch therefore: for ye know not what hour your Lord doth come . . . Therefore be ye also ready: for in such an hour as ye think not the Son of man cometh."

In some believers' minds, since they cannot know when Jesus will return, many are lulled into a deep sleep and become oblivious to the signs of the times.

I will dig deeper into Matthew 24:36-44 below. In order to place those verses into perspective, we must read I Thessalonians 5:1-11.

Clue 3 is found in I Thessalonians 5:1-11 and tells us that an astute believer will be aware when Jesus's return is near. "But of the times and the seasons, brethren, ye have no need that I write unto you. For yourselves know perfectly that the day of the Lord so cometh as a thief in the night. For when they shall say, Peace and safety; then sudden destruction cometh upon them, as travail upon a woman with child; and they shall not escape. But ye, brethren, are not in darkness, that that day should overtake you as a thief."

Let's inject some Jewish cultural perspective in our Christian faith. Matthew 24:36-44 contains a Hebraic idiom.

Let's review.

What is an idiom? An idiom is a group of words established by usage as having a meaning not deducible from those of the individual words (e.g., "rain cats and dogs").

The phrase, "But of that day and hour no one knows, not even the angels of heaven, but My Father only," has deeper meanings. Let's explore the first meaning.

When a bride and groom were married in ancient Jewish custom, they were legally married a year or more before they consummated their marriage. This was called the betrothal period. During this time, the bridegroom prepared a home for his bride.

The groom's father would inspect the home. Once the home met the father's standards, he would instruct the son "go get his bride." The marriage would then be consummated, and the marriage feast would begin.

Jesus's disciple, John, alluded to the above representation in John 14:1-3. "Let not your heart be troubled: ye believe in God, believe also in me. In my Father's house are many mansions: if it were not so, I would have told you. I go to prepare a place for you. And if I go and prepare a place for you, I will come again, and receive you unto myself; that where I am, there ye may be also."

Blood Moon—God's Warning

After the rapture of the church, we will enjoy a marriage supper with Jesus during the seven years of tribulation on the earth. The church will be with Jesus, her bridegroom.

In ancient Jewish marital custom, as the groom prepared the home for his bride, friends would pass by and ask when he would be finished with construction.

The groom would respond, "No one knows the day or the hour, only my father." In other words, "When my father is ready for my bride to join me, I will retrieve my betrothed wife."

Let's explore the second meaning more.

The Feast of Trumpets begins on the first day of a new lunar cycle, and no one could determine the beginning of that cycle until a sliver of the new moon appeared in the sky. So, no one could know the **exact day or hour** Rosh Hashanah, or the coming of Jesus would be.

It is important for you to understand what happens during the Feast of Trumpets. During it, musicians blow their trumpets on many occasions. At the end of the feast, the musicians blast their trumpets ninety times to signify the climax of the feast. One of the last blasts is a climatic one called Teki'ah Gedolah, which means "the Great Blast." It refers to the day of the Lord spoken about in Joel 2 and Acts 2. The blast is long and signifies victory and good news. In the New Testament, this blast is referred to as the Last Trump.

Paul says in his first letter to the Corinthians 15:51-52, "Behold, I shew you a mystery; We shall not all sleep, but we shall all be changed, In a moment, in the twinkling of an eye, at the last trump: for the trumpet shall sound, and the dead shall be raised incorruptible, and we shall be changed."

In Jewish astronomy, as a sliver of white rims the edge of the dark disc of the moon, the moon is considered to represent an eyelid winking and is referred to as a "twinkling of an eye."

Remember, Paul had a Pharisaical background. He would have had full knowledge of Rosh Hashanah, the Feast of Trumpets. He would have known about the Teki'ah Gedolah, the Last Trump.

Following the Feast of Trumpets, ancient Jews observed seven days of affliction. These days lead up to Yom Kippur—the Day of Atonement.

The sixth Jewish fall feast, **Yom Kippur,** also known as the Day of Atonement, is celebrated on the tenth day of Tishri. The third trump of God, called the great trump, is blown during Yom Kippur and serves to warn mankind of the last call to accept God's redemptive plan. Yom Kippur is a foreshadowing of God's last call to accept Jesus as mankind's redemption from sin.

A scapegoat known as *azazel* in Hebrew was used during Yom Kippur. *Azazel*, the scapegoat, was a foreshadowing of Satan. The priest would take the scapegoat and place the sins of the people upon it. The scapegoat would then be sent out of the city.

Review Matthew 24:29-31 below. You will see a stark difference in how the astronomical signs are depicted when compared to the passage in Acts 2 where the moon will turn to blood and the sun to sackcloth.

Blood Moon—God's Warning

"Immediately after the tribulation of those days shall the sun be darkened, and the moon shall not give her light, and the stars shall fall from heaven, and the powers of the heavens shall be shaken: And then shall appear the sign of the Son of man in heaven: and then shall all the tribes of the earth mourn, and they shall see the Son of man coming in the clouds of heaven with power and great glory. And he shall send his angels with a great sound of a trumpet, and they shall gather together his elect from the four winds, from one end of heaven to the other" (Matthew 24:29-31). This passage tells the reader how the skies will proclaim that the end of Yom Kippur is nigh.

Two events will be occurring during the last Yom Kippur of the end times. The first event is the tribulation period.

A one world government will be formed. Its methodology and belief system will rest upon the spirit of antichrist. Today, we can see these antichrist roots coming into springtime. Anti-Jesus propaganda is at an all-time high. What is the reasoning for such hatred towards the Son of God, who showed love by giving His life to provide a pathway to God? Simple: **deception** gifted by the spirit of antichrist.

During the Tribulation Period, Jews will lament rejecting their Messiah, Jesus.

The second event is a joyous event: the "honeymoon" and marriage supper that the faithful and martyred church will enjoy with Jesus. The church will be in fullness of their "marriage" to Jesus. No longer will she be betrothed; the true followers of Jesus will live with Him physically.

As I write these words, I long for that day when toil and pain will be no more for those who have accepted Jesus as Savior and Lord of their lives. This is the hope Jesus offers to every human who has ever lived!

After a Hebrew wedding, the honeymoon would last for seven days. In the Bible, days oftentimes represent years when referring to a spiritual foreshadow. The tribulation period will be seven years, and Jesus's bride, the faithful and martyred church, will enjoy a seven-year honeymoon period. After seven years have been completed, Jesus will then return to earth with His bride, create a new heaven and earth, and rule and reign in the Messianic age known as the Millennium.

The **Feast of Tabernacles,** Festival of Booths or Sukkah, is the last fall Jewish feast. The Messianic age begins at the start of the "last days" Feast of Tabernacles.

Five days after Yom Kippur on the fifteen day of Tishri, the Feast of Tabernacles begins.

The Feast of Tabernacles is a seven day feast and represents the complete reign of Jesus during the Millennium. Remember, seven in the scriptures represents completion.

During the Feast of Tabernacles, God will tabernacle with His redeemed Hebrew people. Jesus will rule and reign over Israel for one thousand years. The words of Jeremiah the prophet will be

Blood Moon—God's Warning

fulfilled when he said, "And they shall be my people, and I will be their God:" (Jeremiah 32:38).

This feast is full of joy. Israel has repented, and now they dwell in full union with God.

The ancient Hebrews mistakenly believed Jesus came to destroy the Hebrew scriptures. Jesus attempted to erase their fears when He said in Matthew 5:17-18, "Think not that I am come to destroy the law, or the prophets: I am not come to destroy, but to fulfil. For verily I say unto you, Till heaven and earth pass, one jot or one tittle shall in no wise pass from the law, till all be fulfilled."

Remember the sixth chapter of Hosea and verse three tells us that the coming of the Messiah, the teacher, would be as the former and latter rain of the earth. We established that Israel's rains occur in the spring, Nisan, and the fall, Tishri. Jesus's first coming correlated with Nisan, and His second coming will correlate with Tishri.

Remember the second chapter of Joel in the twenty-third verse, Joel tells us that the former and latter rain would come in the first month. The Hebrew calendar has two first months, Nisan and Tishri. Joel gave us a clue that Jesus would come to earth in Nisan and Tishri.

Besides giving the watchful believer clues that Jesus would rapture the church during Rosh Hashanah, and that Jesus would make His final appearance in Jerusalem on the Mount of Olives during His Second Coming at the end of Yom Kippur, God provided one more clue—**a tetrad of blood moons.**

J. Nell Brown

Blood moons to Jewish feasts can be viewed as a clock in relationship to an annual calendar. Blood moons allow us to zoom in on important dates.

Chapter 7
Blood Moons

Blood moons are simply lunar eclipses. A lunar eclipse occurs when a full moon passes in the earth's shadow. The moon appears red because the light from the sun is bent due to the earth's atmosphere, causing a band of particles to reflect the light. This is why sunsets in the evening appear red or orange. The band of particles in the earth's atmosphere absorbs some colors of the light spectrum but not others.

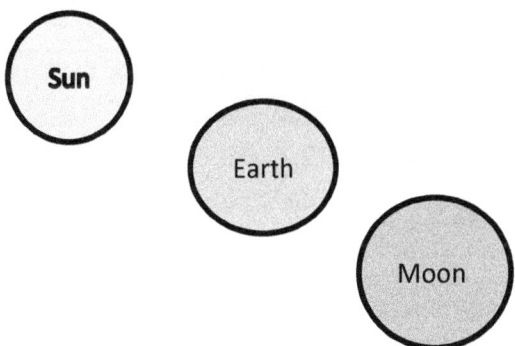

Blood moons are prophesied for the last days in Joel 2 and Acts 2.

The last days refer to the time period after Jesus fulfilled the spring feasts and ascended to heaven.

Joel 2:28-31 says, "And it shall come to pass afterward, that I will pour out my spirit upon all flesh; and your sons and your daughters shall prophesy, your old men shall dream dreams, your young men shall see visions: And also upon the servants and upon the handmaids in those days will I pour out my spirit. I will shew wonders in the heavens and in the earth, blood, and fire, and pillars of smoke. The sun shall be turned into darkness, and the moon into blood, before the great and terrible day of the Lord come." This prophecy began to be fulfilled in Acts 2:17-21.

Some Jewish scholars believe that a blood moon represents Adonai (the Lord) dealing with Israel.

God is a God of order. He demonstrated His nature of order when He created the world from a formless void of darkness. Even numbers in the Bible bear significance.

The number four, or tetrad, in the Bible represents God setting things in order. As a result, the astute believer takes note when a tetrad, a grouping of four, blood moons occurs during Jewish feasts. Now that we understand the Jewish spring and fall feasts, let's place the blood moons in context of these important appointed times.

Jesus's crucifixion occurred in AD 33; Blood moons occurred from AD 32 to AD 33.

* Passover, April 14, 32

* Sukkoth, October 7, 32

Jesus Crucified April 3, 33

Blood Moon—God's Warning

Supernatural crucifixion darkness may have occurred on April 3, 33.

* Passover, April 3, 33
* Sukkoth, September 27, 33

The lunar eclipses of AD 32-33 are questionable for me. I have not been able to find overwhelming research to support their occurrence. However, the dates below are confirmed by NASA.

The Spanish Inquisition began in 1492. Blood moons fell on the dates below.

* Passover, April 2, 1493
* Sukkoth, Sept. 25, 1493
* Passover, March 22, 1494
* Sukkoth, Sept. 15, 1494

On October 12, 1942, Columbus arrived in the Bahamas. Some believe that Christopher Columbus's main purpose for traveling to the Americas was to secure a new homeland for the Jewish people before the Spanish Inquisition began. Whether Columbus was a Jew or not doesn't debunk this hypothesis. Many gentiles, including Corrie ten Boom and American soldiers during World War II, were used by God to assist the Jews during Hitler's Germany.

Israel became a nation after the War of Independence concluded in 1948. This set of four blood moons occurred after the War of Independence. I will explore this phenomenon later.

* Passover, April 13, 1949
* Sukkoth, Oct. 7, 1949

* Passover, April 2, 1950

* Sukkoth, Sept. 26, 1950

Israel's Six-Day War was won in 1967. As a result, Israel reacquired the eastern side of Jerusalem, thus partially fulfilling the prophecy in Ezekiel that Israel would once again possess the city. Some say that Jews don't care if they repossess Jerusalem. The desire of the Jewish people is not relevant in prophecy. Only God's desire and plans are relevant.

For instance, I never desired to write nonfiction or fiction. My desires for my life were and still are very different; however, God's purposes will be accomplished.

* Passover, April 24, 1967

* Sukkoth, October 18, 1967

* Passover, April 13, 1968

* Sukkoth, October 6, 1968

On June 7, 1967 Jerusalem was recaptured.

Finally, we have arrived to our very own time—2014 to 2015. What does God have in store for us?

* Passover, April 15, 2014

* Sukkoth, October 8, 2014

* Passover, April 4, 2015

* Sukkoth, September 28, 2015

If we review Joel 2 and Acts 2, we will see that these passages also speak of the sun going dark. The sun going dark seems to suggest a solar eclipse.

Blood Moon—God's Warning

A solar eclipse occurs when the moon passes in between the earth and the sun. A solar eclipse cannot be seen from all points on earth because of the tilt of the earth.

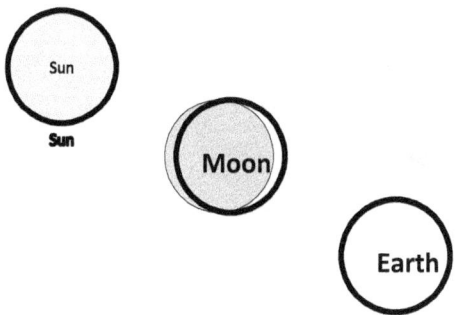

In Jewish astronomy, it is thought that God is dealing with the gentile nations when a solar eclipse occurs on a Jewish feast.

It is interesting to note that a solar eclipse will fall on the Jewish religious New Year, March 20, 2015, and on Rosh Hashanah, the Feast of Trumpets, on September 13, 2015.

I am not one to give any credence to predictions; however, I would not complain if Jesus's return is tomorrow or September 13, 2015!

The Jewish religious New Year begins in Nisan 5775. The Hebrew year 5775 correlates with Gregorian year of 2014-2015.

Passover of 2014 occurs in Nisan on April 15. A blood moon will occur on this day. Tax day may be interesting!

The Feast of Tabernacle, Sukkoth, occurs on October 8, 2014. A blood moon will occur on this day.

The Jewish religious New Year begins in 2015 on March 20. A solar eclipse will occur on this day.

Passover of 2015 occurs in the month of Nisan on April 4. A blood moon will appear on this day.

The Jewish civil New Year begins in the month of Tishri. The 2015 civil New Year will begin with a total solar eclipse, and two weeks later, a total lunar eclipse coinciding with the Feast of Tabernacles will occur.

The Feast of Trumpets, Rosh Hashanah, occurs on September (Tishri) 13, 2015. A solar eclipse will occur that day. Could this be the day of the rapture?

Let's live like Jesus is coming. Run your race diligently.

Lastly, the Feast of Tabernacles will occur September 28, 2015. A blood moon will occur on that day. Will Jesus begin His tabernacle with the Jewish people?

Jesus was a Torah-observant Jewish citizen. He communicated many times to His audience in Hebraic idioms and parables. He spoke with precision. He never wasted a word. Was Jesus warning us of the blood moons of 2014-2015?

Only the blood moon occurring on September 28, 2015 will be visible from Jerusalem. However, if we review the tetrad of blood moons of 1949-1950 and 1967-1968, we will realize that only the blood moons occurring on the first three Jewish feasts (Passover on April 13, 1949, Sukkoth on October 7, 1949, and Passover on April 2, 1950) were visible from Jerusalem, yet they were significant events that affected the Jewish people.

Blood Moon—God's Warning

God delivers messages to every person in relationship with Him. "Surely the Lord GOD does nothing, Unless He reveals His secret to His servants the prophets" (Amos 3:7).

We will find out soon enough.

Please read Matthew chapter 24, paying special attention to verse fourteen. "And this gospel of the kingdom shall be preached in all the world for a witness unto all nations; and then shall the end come."

In light of this verse, God allowed me to write The God Factor Saga series. Learn more about it and book one, *Frozen Prayers*, below.

Thank you for reading.

J. Nell Brown

Reader Question:

"In chapter 4, the section on Passover, you say that Jesus was sacrificed at the same time that the Passover lambs were being killed. Each gospel says that Jesus ate the Passover with his disciples before going to the Garden of Gethsemane, which would have meant that the Passover lambs would have already been sacrificed. Could you clarify this for me? This seems contradictory to me. Thank you!"

Answer:

Let's get started!

I'd like to use Matthew's and John's accounts of Passover and The Feast of Unleavened Bread during Jesus's passion. A few facts to review: the Jewish day begins in the evening at 18:00 and continues through midnight to 18:00 the next evening.

For instance, 18:00 on Thursday to 18:00 on Friday equals one day.

Passover is a twenty-four hour feast. Using our example above, Passover would start Thursday at 18:00 and continue to 18:00 on Friday. Whereas, the Feast of Unleavened Bread can last up to seven days.

The big clue for us is in Matthew 26:17. "Now the **first** day of the feast of **unleavened bread** the disciples came to Jesus, saying unto him, Where wilt thou that we prepare for thee to eat the passover?"

When does Passover begin? In a some commentaries that study Matthew 26:17, the Passover and Feast of Unleavened Bread can be used to describe the combination of the 14th day of Nisan (Passover) and the subsequent week long Feast of Unleavened Bread. In essence, making the first day of the Feast of Unleavened Bread the 14th day of Nisan, or Passover.

Confusing? I agree. But, let's see if we can clarify.

Matthew 26:17 seems to say that the Passover lamb would be slain on the 1st day of the Feast of Unleavened Bread, the 15th day of Nisan. In reality, this first day really means the 14th day of Nisan. Let's look at the evidence.

John 18:28: "Then led they Jesus from Caiaphas unto the hall of judgment: and it was early; and they themselves went not into the judgment hall, lest they should be defiled; but that they might eat the passover." The Jews hadn't eaten their Passover sader.

Exodus 12:6: "And ye shall keep it up until the fourteenth day of the same month: and the whole assembly of the congregation of Israel shall kill it in the **evening**." The evening would be the afternoon of the fourteen.

Exodus 12:8: "And they shall eat the flesh in that night [night=after midnight, early morning hours], roast with fire, and unleavened bread; and with bitter herbs they shall eat it." We can see from this verse the unleavened bread has already been prepared.

The contradiction seems to occur in these verses as well.

Exodus 12:18: "In the first month, on the fourteenth day of the month at even, ye shall eat unleavened bread, until the one and twentieth day of the month at even."

Leviticus 23:5: "In the fourteenth day of the first month at **even** is the Lord's passover."

Leviticus 23:6: "And on the fifteenth day of the same month is the feast of unleavened bread unto the LORD: seven days ye must eat unleavened bread."

The Hebrew for **evening** in Exodus 12:6 and Leviticus 23:5 literally reads "between the evenings." The first of these two evenings is when the sun begins its descent from its zenith at noon, and the second when the sun sets at 18:00. So "between the evenings" refers to between noon and 18:00 or 3 PM (15:00), which is also called the ninth hour.

The ninth hour on the 14th of Nisan is when the Messiah was prophesied to die. However, the Jews still hadn't eaten the Passover lamb according to John 18:28. They would eat the roast the night of the 15th of Nisan. Yet, according to Exodus 12:18, unleavened bread would be eaten beginning on the 14th of Nisan, known as the Lord's Passover. This meal, according to the Bible and other commentaries, included bread and grape juice, but no roasted lamb. The Passover lamb hadn't been slain yet, but would be later that day at about 3 PM at the same time Jesus would be crucified.

Let's evaluate the Hebrew Scriptures to see if the New Testament rendering of two times for lamb sacrifice coincides with the Hebrew Scriptures. Exodus 29:39 reads, "The one lamb thou shalt offer in the morning, and the other lamb thou shalt offer at even."

Blood Moon—God's Warning

Even here means "between the evenings" or 15:00 (3 PM). The Jewish historian Josephus confirms that the Passover lambs were slain from the ninth hour to the eleventh hour, that being from 3 PM to 5 PM. He writes in *Wars of the Jews*, Book VI, Chapter IX, Section 3: "So these high priests, upon the coming of that feast which is called the Passover, when they slay their sacrifices, from the ninth hour till the eleventh, but so that a company not less than ten belong to every sacrifice ..."

In conclusion, lambs were killed in the morning, but there is no evidence that Jesus and His disciples partook of lamb roast during the Lord's Supper (Passover), which occurred in the morning before 9:00 AM when Jesus was crucified and 3 PM, at the end of the 14th day of Nisan, when Jesus died. I tend to think that the presence of a lamb of roast at the Lord's Supper would have been redundant since Jesus was present at the meal and stressed the importance of the bread and the cup.

The confusion begins in the New Testament, when at times Passover on the 14th of Nisan is overlaid with the Feast of Unleavened Bread, which typically starts on the 15th day of Nisan.

Therefore, the two events—the time for the killing of the Passover lamb and the death of Jesus—coincided precisely on Friday afternoon at 3 PM of the 14th of Nisan—the Lord's Passover.

Studying the timing of the original Passover may help.

Exodus 12:29: "And it came to pass, that at midnight the LORD smote all the firstborn in the land of Egypt."

J. Nell Brown

Numbers 33:3: "And they departed from Rameses in the first month, on the fifteenth day of the first month; on the morrow after the passover the children of Israel went out with an high hand in the sight of all the Egyptians."

These passages show that the slaying of Egypt's firstborn occurred at midnight on the 15th of Nisan, making sense of the reference in John 18:28 where the Passover meal of roasted lamb is eaten in the early hours of 15th of Nisan. The Paschal lamb, a symbol of Jesus, had been slain a few hours earlier on the afternoon of 14th of Nisan at 3 PM. Jesus had eaten the Lord's Supper with his disciples before 9:00 AM on the 14th of Nisan.

As a result, Matthew 26:17, Mark 14:12, and Luke 22:1, 7-8 are actually referring to the 14th of Nisan by calling it the first day of the feast of unleavened bread, even though according to Leviticus the feast would be celebrated on the 15th of Nisan.

Our final attempt is a timeline.

The 14th day of Nisan (from 18:00 to 9:00): "Then came the day of unleavened bread, when the passover must be killed" (Luke 22:7).

Later on the 14th day of Nisan (from 18:00 to 9:00): Preparation for the Passover is discussed in Matthew 26:17-19, Mark 14:12-16, and Luke 22:7-13.

Later on the 14th day of Nisan (from 18:00 to 9:00), probably just after sunset, Jesus celebrated the Passover meal of unleavened bread and wine with His disciples. The roasted lamb

Blood Moon—God's Warning

wasn't ready and would be eaten after the crucifixion, according to John.

Jesus retires to Gethsemane and is arrested: Matthew 26:30-56, Mark 14:26-52, Luke 22:39-53, and John 18:1-12.

In the early morning hours but still during Passover Day on the 14th of Nisan, the trials, scouring, and torture took place.

At 9:00 AM, the third hour (according to Mark 15:25), the crucifixion began.

Jesus died at the very moment the Passover Lamb would be slain in the temple, the ninth hour, 3 PM on the 14th day of Nisan.

Some scholars believe that the first day would be counted by ancient Hebrews as the moment Jesus was laid in the tomb until the sunset around 18:00 beginning the next day, the 15th day of Nisan. But, this point is shaky at best.

J. Nell Brown

Dear Reader,

Thoughtful Amazon reviews about an author's work are like a pay raise or a tip to employees in traditional jobs. If you enjoyed this essay, please take a moment to place a review on Amazon.com, sharing with other readers what you learned. Your feedback is invaluable.

A21 Campaign, a charity for human-trafficked children, is my charity of choice for a percentage of the proceeds from my novels.

I look forward to saying "hello" to you on Facebook. Please like my page at www.facebook.com/JNellBrown, so you may keep up with my writing journey.

With gratitude,

J. Nell Brown

Blood Moon—God's Warning

Begin the adventure in J. Nell Brown's God Factor Saga book one, *Frozen Prayers*.

When we sleep at night, our brains lull into disorganized patterns of peaks and troughs, but when the only child of missionaries sleeps, she stares into the past and future, unlocking ancient mysteries God had hidden before He created the universe, mysteries meant to warn His children of a cataclysmic event that will resemble a pandemic.

J. Nell Brown

Books by

J. Nell Brown

Nonfiction

Shhh, My Father Is Speaking, and I Am Listening: A Bible Study on Hearing God's Voice

Blood Moon—God's Warning: Why Knowledge of Jewish Feasts Is Essential to Understand the Blood Moons of 2014 and 2015

Fiction

God Factor Saga Series EBooks:

House Guest: A Short Story

A Generation of Lighted Evergreens: A Novella

Frozen Prayers

Blood Moon Relics

Autumn Rains: A Winter Adventure Love Story

The Rose of A.D. 30: A Trilogy

Collector's First Edition Paperback
The Omega Journey: Blood Moons Whisper

A Generation of Lighted Evergreens: A Novella

Coming January 2016

God Factor Saga Series Book 4: *Desert Places*

Acknowledgements

Special thanks to my late father Chaplain Austin Brown, my mother Mrs. Jeanette Brown, and my sisters JaWanda Thacker, Major Austine Rawllins, and Rosa Lee Brown, JD.

To Susan and Jo, my invisible copyeditors, thank you for your eagles' eyes.

J. Nell Brown

Author Biography

J. Nell Brown, daughter of a chaplain and a teacher, is a Florida native.

Her relationship with Yeshua mixed with experiences in life, travel, extensive Bible study, and peoples' stories blend together to form characters, plots, and geographical settings for her novels. An involuntary insomniac, Brown practices medicine and writes in her free time.

She is a self-proclaimed nerd and loves all things scientific. Her love of science is demonstrated by her research at Los Alamos National Laboratory, the site for the development of the atomic bomb. She graduated with honors from The University of Florida (U of F) College of Agriculture and received her medical doctorate from the same. After completing an anesthesia residency at The University of Chicago Hospitals, she practices in Florida.

Her heart overflows with compassion for hurting people, particularly children. A portion of the proceeds from this book will go to A21 Campaign, a rescue charity for human trafficked children, and Eastside Baptist School in Gainesville, Florida. Eastside is a

Blood Moon—God's Warning

school of love, values, and solid educational curriculum for children whose parents would not be able to afford an alternative school education.

Kindredfriendships.com, a project designed for adventurous women in need of spiritual renewal, was founded by J. Nell Brown in 2008.

Shhh, My Father Is Speaking, and I Am Listening is the title of her first nonfiction book, and the Bible is her favorite literary masterpiece. You may follow J. Nell Brown on her author website JNellBrown.com.

The God Factor Saga Series begins in book one, *Frozen Prayers*, and continues in book two, *Blood Moon Relics*, a thriller and suspense novel.

Book three, *Autumn Rains*, continues the story and is a moving winter love tale that deals with bravery, surrendering to God, and redemption.

Book four, *Desert Places*, picks up the pace again and throws the characters into another adventure of mystery and intrigue while they deal with infertility, adultery and financial woes.

Thank you for reading this essay!

You may purchase *The Omega Journey* on Amazon.com and www.JNellBrown.com. Should you desire an autographed copy, you may purchase a paperback from JNellBrown.com or Amazon.com under the "other options" tab.

www.ingramcontent.com/pod-product-compliance
Lightning Source LLC
Chambersburg PA
CBHW031209020426
42333CB00013B/860